Slip-Stitch Knits

SHERYL THIES

Slip-Stitch
KNITS

Simple Colorwork Cowls,
Scarves, and Shawls

Martingale®
Create with Confidence

Slip-Stitch Knits:
Simple Colorwork Cowls, Scarves, and Shawls
© 2015 by Sheryl Thies

Martingale®
19021 120th Ave. NE, Ste. 102
Bothell, WA 98011-9511 USA
ShopMartingale.com

Printed in China
20 19 18 17 16 15   8 7 6 5 4 3 2 1

Library of Congress Cataloging-in-Publication Data
is available upon request.

ISBN: 978-1-60468-540-4

MISSION STATEMENT

Dedicated to providing quality products and service
to inspire creativity.

CREDITS

PUBLISHER AND CHIEF VISIONARY OFFICER
Jennifer Erbe Keltner

EDITORIAL DIRECTOR
Karen Costello Soltys

ACQUISITIONS EDITOR
Karen M. Burns

TECHNICAL EDITOR
Ursula Reikes

COPY EDITOR
Sheila Chapman Ryan

DESIGN DIRECTOR
Paula Schlosser

PHOTOGRAPHER
Brent Kane

PRODUCTION MANAGER
Regina Girard

COVER AND INTERIOR DESIGNER
Adrienne Smitke

ILLUSTRATORS
Kathryn Conway and
Cheryl Fall

DEDICATION

To my good neighbor and treasured friend Eileen.

She freely shares her eye for a tasteful style, generously offers spontaneous supper invitations, and is my cheerleader in the corner who knows just when to commiserate and when to push me forward. It's a pleasure to be her partner in crime in all our thrilling and humorous adventures—like joining a 100-piece accordion band.

Contents

Introduction   9

Creating Color Patterns   11

SCARVES   17

   Glacial Ridge   18

   Hawks Landing   20

   Thunder Hollow Run   23

   Breeze Point   26

   Moonlight Terrace   28

   Token Creek   32

COWLS   35

   Quarry Hill Circle   36

   Meadowbrook Loop   40

   Cannonball Trail   42

SHAWLS   45

   Mallow Flower Lane   46

   Moraine View   50

   Yahara Bay   54

Start and Finish Like a Pro   59

Useful Information   61

Abbreviations and Glossary   62

Resources   62

Acknowledgments   63

About the Author   64

Introduction

We live in a colorful world. Pause a moment and look around. Color is everywhere. Take in the multiple shades of a blue-gray sky, the varying colors of the earth we stand on, and the colors of the fabric of our clothing. Color is even in our vocabulary. Ever been tickled pink? Who's the black sheep in your family? Received inspiration out of the blue?

We don't have to understand the science behind color, nor do we need to know the difference between hue, tint, shade, and tone, to know which colors we like and which ones we don't. Ever since receiving our first pack of crayons, we've been adding our favorite colors to our surroundings. Sometimes we follow society's norms and color inside the lines, while other times we prefer the freedom of coloring outside the lines.

Slip-stitch knitting combines the best of coloring between and outside the lines. Although the patterns created appear complex, the process is uncomplicated. Using only one color of yarn across a row, stitches are knit, purled, or slipped. The slipped stitches pull the color from the previous row up into the row being worked.

Slipping stitches is not a new technique, but thanks to the revolutionary ideas of Barbara Walker, slip-stitch colorwork was elevated to a new level. In the 1970s she coined the term *mosaic knitting* for her new class of knitting. Before the introduction of her groundbreaking work, color was added to projects using the Fair Isle or stranded method. You may have seen this method used in Scandinavian ski sweaters and accessories. With the Fair Isle method, experienced knitters work with two strands of yarn across a row, carrying the yarn not in use behind the stitches being worked, to create a bulky fabric prone to puckering.

Even relatively new knitters can enjoy the simplicity of mosaic or slip-stitch knitting and achieve impressive results. The scarves, cowls, and shawls included here require little or no shaping and only basic knitting skills. If you're confident with knitting and purling, you're ready to give slip-stitch knitting a try.

Make your knitting world more colorful with this simple technique. Your friends will be green with envy when they see your lovely multihued creations.

~ *Sheryl*

Creating Color Patterns

Adding color to your knitting is as easy as knitting stripes using one color of yarn at a time, yet the results are far more dramatic and appear complex. Thanks to the simple technique of slipping stitches, you can easily create fascinating color patterns. If you know how to knit and purl, you are ready to slip some color into your knitting.

Slipping a Stitch

When using slipped stitches to create a color pattern in your knitting, a single color is worked across two rows, a right-side row and a wrong-side row. The yarn is then dropped and left to dangle along the edge, while the contrasting color is used to work across the next two rows. By slipping stitches as you work across a row, the color not in use is pulled up into the row being worked, creating an elongated stitch and adding another color to the row.

In general, the yarns are alternated every two rows and carried up the side of the work. (There are two patterns in this book, however, Hawks Landing on page 20 and Yahara Bay on page 54, in which a single color is worked across four rows.) Don't cut the yarn when you reach the end of the two-row stint. To change the yarn color, finish the wrong-side row and turn to the right side of the work. The color being dropped should hang toward the front or right side of the work. Pick up the new color and bring it up behind the color just dropped.

Let old color hang toward the front along the side edge and pick up the new color behind the dropped yarn.

Hold the yarn in back when slipping stitches, with the right-side rows facing you.

Hold the yarn in front when slipping stitches, with the wrong-side rows facing you.

To work a slip stitch, move a stitch from the left needle to the right needle without working the stitch. Simply insert the tip of the right-hand needle into the next stitch as if you were going to purl the stitch and slide the stitch off the left-hand needle onto the right-hand needle. All slip stitches are slipped purlwise. The slipped stitch will always be the color not in use. And only one or two (at the most) stitches are slipped consecutively. The rows can be worked in either knit or purl stitches or a combination of both. And the rows can be worked back and forth or in the round.

While slipping a stitch, the yarn is always held on the wrong side of the work, which means it will either be held in the back on a right-side row or in the front on a wrong-side row.

To avoid any confusion, the slip-stitch patterns include where to hold the yarn while slipping the stitch. Abbreviations are used for the terms "with yarn in front" (wyif) and "with yarn in back" (wyib).

Reading a Slip-Stitch Pattern Chart

Several of the projects include a chart for the slip-stitch pattern, giving a visual representation of the pattern. Once you're familiar with reading charts, you may find the charted directions easier to follow than line-by-line written directions.

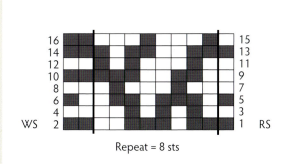

Repeat = 8 sts

Legend

Sl all sts pw

= A. When first st in row is black, work sts as follows:
RS: K black squares, sl white squares wyib
WS: P black squares, sl white squares wyif

= B. When first st in row is white, work sts as follows:
RS: K white squares, sl black squares wyib
WS: K white squares, sl black squares wyif

A slip-stitch pattern chart used to make the scarf seen top right (Token Creek, page 32).

Compare the photo to the chart at left and begin to visualize the stitch pattern.

The chart is read beginning with the first row at the bottom. Right-side rows are odd-numbered rows and are read from right to left. The wrong-side rows are even-numbered rows and are read from left to right. However, when working in the round, all rows are read from right to left.

Each horizontal row of squares on the chart represents two rows of knitting, a right-side *and* a wrong-side row. The rows are mirror images of each other. The odd numbers along the right edge of the chart represent the right-side row and the even numbers along the left edge of the chart represent the wrong side of the work.

The first stitch, either a black or a white square, indicates the color used for the next row. On all rows that begin with a black square, you work the black squares and slip the white squares. On all rows that begin with a white square, you work the white squares and slip the black squares.

Because the wrong-side row is a mirror image of the right-side row, you can read your work and not have to read the chart. Work the stitches in the same color as the working yarn and slip the slipped stitches from the previous row. When working back and forth in stockinette stitch, purl the purl stitches; when working in garter stitch, knit the purl stitches. The exception is when working in the round for stockinette stitch, where you'll knit all the knit stitches on every round.

The two vertical lines near the side edges are the pattern repeat lines. The stitches outside the repeat lines are the edge stitches and only worked at the beginning and end of the row, while the stitches within the repeat lines are repeated across the row.

CHART TIP

When reading a chart, many people photocopy the chart and put it on a magnetic board, then use a magnetic bar or a ruler below the row to keep track of the row they're working on. But rather than covering up the part of the chart you've already worked, place the bar above the row you're ready to work to cover up the part that's yet to come since those stitches don't yet exist on your knitting. Pay attention to how the stitches you're working line up with the stitches from the previous row to avoid mistakes. If you're working directly from the book, you can use a sticky note above the row.

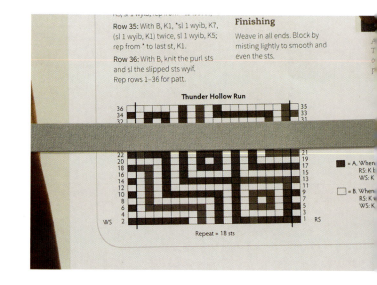

Remember, the color of the first square of every row indicates the color for that row.

Associated with each chart is a legend that indicates what is done with each stitch. Be sure to check the legend before working to fully understand how the stitches are to be worked.

Making a Swatch

Slipping stitches pulls the fabric in widthwise a bit more than just knitting or purling. In the patterns, the suggested needle size is usually several sizes larger than the needle size indicated on the yarn label. Work a swatch in the slip-stitch pattern, block it by misting, and let the swatch dry *before* measuring to calculate the gauge. Adjust your needle size if necessary.

As you work the swatch, you'll become familiar with the pattern, which may help avoid problems later on. Practice using the swatch to read the row of stitches on your needle and compare the row to the slip-stitch pattern or chart. This is particularly helpful in the event you lose your place and have to find the correct row. Also note that the alternating color rows create a stripe pattern on the wrong side and you can count the two-row stripes to determine which row you should be working.

Adjust the needle size if necessary to achieve the stated gauge.

SCARVES

FINISHED MEASUREMENTS

9" x 52"

MATERIALS

A 2 skeins of Martha Stewart Crafts Extra Soft Wool Blend from Lion Brand Yarns (65% acrylic, 35% wool; 3.5 oz/100 g; 164 yds/ 100 m) in color 550 Gray Pearl (4)

B 1 skein of Amazing from Lion Brand Yarns (53% wool, 47% acrylic; 1.75 oz/50 g; 147 yds/ 135 m) in color 208 Glacier Bay (4)

Size 10 (6 mm) needles or size required to obtain gauge

GAUGE

16 sts = 4" in sl-st patt

GLACIAL RIDGE

A perfect complement to your cool-weather wardrobe, this scarf adds a soft touch of color and will keep the chill away. The garter-stitch dashes and interesting side nubs add texture.

Slip-Stitch Pattern

(Multiple of 6 sts + 7 sts)

Use cable CO method (page 59) to CO number of sts specified in scarf instructions.

Sl all sts pw.

Row 1 (RS): With A, CO 3 sts, BO 3 sts, knit to end of row.

Row 2: With A, CO 3 sts, BO 3 sts, K2, purl to last 3 sts, K3.

Row 3: With B, K3, *sl 1 wyib, K5; rep from * to last 4 sts, sl 1 wyib, K3.

Row 4: With B, K3, *sl 1 wyif, K5; rep from * to last 4 sts, sl 1 wyif, K3.

Row 5: With A, CO 3 sts, BO 3 sts, knit to end of row.

Row 6: With A, CO 3 sts, BO 3 sts, K3, purl to last 3 sts, K3.

Row 7: With B, K6, *sl 1 wyib, K5; rep from * to last 7 sts, sl 1 wyib, K6.

Row 8: With B, K6, *sl 1 wyif, K5; rep from * to last 7 sts, sl 1 wyif, K6.

Rep rows 1–8 for patt.

Scarf Instructions

Carry unused yarn up side of work. Do not cut yarn after color change.

With A, use cable CO method to CO 37 sts.

Rows 1–4: Knit.

Patt rows: Work in sl-st patt until piece measures 51", ending with row 6.

Next 4 rows: With A, knit.

BO all sts loosely.

Finishing

Weave in all ends. Block by misting lightly to smooth and even the sts.

HAWKS LANDING

Make a sophisticated statement with this generously-sized ribbed and cabled scarf. Suitable for the well-dressed gentlemen as well as the fashionable woman.

FINISHED MEASUREMENTS

10" x 70"

MATERIALS

Falk from Dale Garn
(100% pure new wool;
1.75 oz/50 g; 116 yds/
106 m) (2)

A 4 skeins in color 5762
Steel

B 1 skein in color 6031
Pewter

Size 7 (4.5 mm) needles or size
required to obtain gauge

1 extra needle (for 3-needle BO)

Cable needle

GAUGE

20 st = 4" in 6 x 2 rib

2 x 2 Rib

(Multiple of 4 sts + 2 sts)

Row 1 (RS): P2, *K2, P2; rep from * to end of row.

Row 2: K2, *P2, K2; rep from * to end of row.

Rep rows 1 and 2 for patt.

6 x 2 Rib

(Multiple of 8 sts + 2 sts)

Row 1 (RS): P2, *K6, P2; rep from * to end of row.

Row 2: K2, *P6, K2; rep from * to end of row.

Rep rows 1 and 2 for patt.

2-Color Cable Rib

(Multiple of 8 sts + 2 sts)

Sl all sts pw.

Setup rows 1 and 2 in scarf instructions must be worked prior to starting this patt.

Row 1 (RS): With A, P2, *sl 1 wyib and drop extra wrap, K4, sl 1 wyib and drop extra wrap, P2; rep from * to end of row.

Row 2: With A, K2, *sl 1 wyif, P4, sl 1 wyif, K2; rep from * to end of row.

Row 3: With A, P2, *sl 1 wyib, K4, sl 1 wyib, P2; rep from * to end of row.

Row 4: With A, K2, *sl 1 wyif, P4, sl 1 wyif, K2; rep from * to end of row.

Row 5: With B, P2, *place sl st on cn and hold in front of work, K2, K1 from cn, sl next 2 sts to cn and hold in back, K1, K2 from cn, P2; rep from * to end of row.

Row 6: With B, K2, *P1 and wrap twice, P4, P1 and wrap twice, K2; rep from * to end of row.

Rep rows 1–6 for patt.

Contrasting colored cables define this classic ribbed scarf.

Scarf Instructions

Make 2 pieces.

Carry unused yarn up side of work. Do not cut yarn after color change.

With A, CO 50 sts.

2 x 2 rib rows: Beg with RS row, work 2 x 2 rib until piece measures 1½" from CO, ending with row 2.

6 x 2 rib rows: Work 6 x 2 rib until piece measures 3" from CO, ending with row 2.

Setup row 1 (RS): With B, P2, *K6, P2; rep from * to end of row.

Setup row 2: With B, K2, *P1 and wrap twice, P4, P1 and wrap twice, K2; rep from * to end of row.

2-color cable rows: Work 2-color cable until piece measures approx 14" from CO, ending with row 5.

Next WS row: With B, K2, *P6, K2; rep from * to end of row.

6 x 2 rib rows: With A, beg with row 1, work 6 x 2 rib until piece measures 35" from CO when slightly stretched, ending with row 2.

Place sts on extra needle and set aside. Make second piece same as first.

3-needle BO: Place half the sts on one needle and half on a second needle. With RS tog, hold both needles in LH. Using extra needle, insert needle into first stitch on front needle, and then into first stitch on back needle; knit 2 sts tog. Repeat with next 2 sts on LH needle; then BO loosely in usual manner. Continue knitting 2 sts tog from front and back needles and BO across row. When 1 st rem on RH needle, cut tail and pass it through last lp.

Knit together 1 stitch from front needle and 1 stitch from back.

Bind off.

Finishing

Weave in ends. Block by misting lightly to smooth and even the sts.

THUNDER HOLLOW RUN

Worked in garter stitch, this no-frills, beefy, and cozy scarf is ready for anything, anywhere, any time. Make one for him and one for yourself.

FINISHED MEASUREMENTS

9" x 60"

MATERIALS

Encore Worsted from Plymouth Yarn Company, Inc. (75% acrylic, 25% wool; 100 g; 200 yds) (4)

A 1 skein in color 688 Coffee Heather

B 1 skein in color 240 Taupe

Size 10 (6 mm) needles or size required to obtain gauge

GAUGE

17 sts = 4" in sl-st patt

Slip-Stitch Pattern

(Multiple of 18 sts + 2 sts)

Sl all sts pw.

Row 1 (RS): With A, K1, *K7, (sl 1 wyib, K1) twice, sl 1 wyib, K6; rep from * to last st, K1.

Row 2 and all WS rows: With color from previous row, knit the purl sts and sl the slipped sts wyif.

Row 3: With B, K1, *sl 1 wyib, K5, (sl 1 wyib, K1) twice, sl 1 wyib, K7; rep from * to last st, K1.

Row 5: With A, K1, *K1, sl 1 wyib, K3, (sl 1 wyib, K1) twice, sl 1 wyib, K7, sl 1 wyib; rep from * to last st, K1.

Row 7: With B, K1, *(sl 1 wyib, K1) 4 times, sl 1 wyib, K7, sl 1 wyib, K1; rep from * to last st, K1.

Row 9: With A, K1, *K1, sl 1 wyib, K3, sl 1 wyib, K1, sl 1 wyib, K7, sl 1 wyib, K1, sl 1 wyib; rep from * to last st, K1.

Row 11: With B, K1, *sl 1 wyib, K5, sl 1 wyib, K7, (sl 1 wyib, K1) twice; rep from * to last st, K1.

Row 13: With A, K1, *K13, (sl 1 wyib, K1) twice, sl 1 wyib; rep from * to last st, K1.

Row 15: With B, K1, *K6, sl 1 wyib, K5, (sl 1 wyib, K1) 3 times; rep from * to last st, K1.

Row 17: With A, K1, *K5, sl 1 wyib, K1, sl 1 wyib, K3, (sl 1 wyib, K1) twice, sl 1 wyib, K2; rep from * to last st, K1.

Row 19: With B, K1, *K4, (sl 1 wyib, K1) 5 times, sl 1 wyib, K3; rep from * to last st, K1.

Row 21: With A, K1, *K3, (sl 1 wyib, K1) twice, sl 1 wyib, K3, sl 1 wyib, K1, sl 1 wyib, K4; rep from * to last st, K1.

Row 23: With B, K1, *K2, (sl 1 wyib, K1) twice, sl 1 wyib, K5, sl 1 wyib, K5; rep from * to last st, K1.

Row 25: With A, K1, *(K1, sl 1 wyib) 3 times, K12; rep from * to last st, K1.

Row 27: With B, K1, *(sl 1 wyib, K1) twice, sl 1 wyib, K7, sl 1 wyib, K5; rep from * to last st, K1.

Row 29: With A, K1, *(K1, sl 1 wyib) twice, K7, sl 1 wyib, K1, sl 1 wyib, K3, sl 1 wyib; rep from * to last st, K1.

Row 31: With B, K1, *sl 1 wyib, K1, sl 1 wyib, K7, (sl 1 wyib, K1) 4 times; rep from * to last st, K1.

Row 33: With A, K1, *K1, sl 1 wyib, K7, (sl 1 wyib, K1) twice, sl 1 wyib, K3, sl 1 wyib; rep from * to last st, K1.

Row 35: With B, K1, *sl 1 wyib, K7, (sl 1 wyib, K1) twice, sl 1 wyib, K5; rep from * to last st, K1.

Row 36: With B, knit the purl sts and sl the slipped sts wyif.
Rep rows 1–36 for patt.

Scarf Instructions

Carry unused yarn up side of work. Do not cut yarn after color change.

With A, CO 38 sts.

Rows 1 (RS) and 2: Knit.

Rows 3 and 4: With B, knit.

Patt rows: Work in sl-st patt until piece measures approx 60", ending with row 36.

Next 2 rows: With A, knit.

BO all sts loosely.

Finishing

Weave in all ends. Block by misting lightly to smooth and even the sts.

Add a little warmth with Thunder Hollow Run. Wear it over a blazer, rugged wear, or a preppy sweater.

Thunder Hollow Run

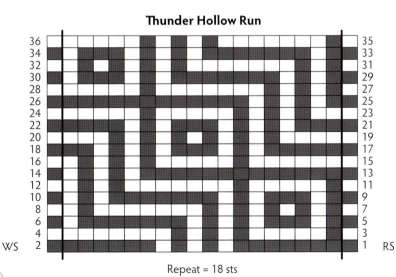

Repeat = 18 sts

Legend

Sl all sts pw

■ = A. When first st in row is black, work sts as follows:
RS: K black squares, sl white squares wyib
WS: K black squares, sl white squares wyif

□ = B. When first st in row is white, work sts as follows:
RS: K white squares, sl black squares wyib
WS: K white squares, sl black squares wyif

FINISHED MEASUREMENTS

5" x 50", excluding fringe

MATERIALS

Lille Lerke by Dale Garn
(53% merino wool,
47% cotton; 1.75 oz/50 g;
154 yds/142 m) (1)

A 1 skein in color 4026
(soft red)

B 1 skein in color 0020
(natural)

Size 6 (4 mm) needles or size
required to obtain gauge

GAUGE

5 sts = 1" in sl-st patt

BREEZE POINT

*Breeze through the day with this attractive color-pattern scarf.
The distinctive loopy fringe gives an artful hint of pizzazz, the
consummate accessory whenever you're out and about.*

Slip-Stitch Pattern

(Multiple of 31 sts)

Sl all sts pw.

Rows 1 (RS), 2, 5, 6, 9, 10, 13, and 14: With A, knit.

Rows 3 and 7: With B, K1, (K1, sl 1 wyib) 4 times, K9, (sl 1 wyib, K1) 3 times, sl 1 wyib, K6.

Rows 4 and 8: With B, K5, (K1, sl 1 wyif) 4 times, P9, (sl 1 wyif, K1) 3 times, sl 1 wyif, K2.

Rows 11 and 15: With B, K10, (sl 1 wyib, K1) 3 times, sl 1 wyib, K14.

Rows 12 and 16: With B, K5, P9, (sl 1 wyif, K1) 3 times, sl 1 wyif, P10.

Rep rows 1–16 for patt.

Scarf Instructions

Carry unused yarn up side of work. Do not cut yarn after color change.

With A, CO 31 sts.

Rows 1 (RS) and 2: Knit.

Rows 3 and 4: With B, knit.

Patt rows: Work in sl-st patt until piece measures approx 50", ending with row 10.

Next 2 rows: With B, knit 2 rows.

Next 2 rows: With A, knit 2 rows.

BO 26 sts loosely and fasten off. Use rem 5 sts for fringe.

Finishing

Create fringe by unraveling 5 rem sts down to CO edge. Make an overhand knot in each fringe and slide knot toward knit edge.

Weave in all ends. Block by misting to smooth and even the sts.

FINISHED MEASUREMENTS

11" x 54"

MATERIALS

Di Lusso from Mango Moon
Yarns (48% silk, 45%
viscose, 4% lamé, 3% nylon;
50 g; 65 yds) **(5)**

A 3 skeins in color 5505
   Orion

B 1 skein in color 5502
   Midnight

C 1 skein in color 5503
   Moonlight

Size 10½ (6.5 mm) circular
needle (24" long) or size
required to obtain gauge

Size K-10½ (6.5 mm) crochet
hook

GAUGE

13 sts = 4" in sl-st patt

MOONLIGHT TERRACE

Get wrapped up in fun and make any outfit special with this beautiful scallop-edged scarf. The touch of sparkle in the yarn hints at merriment and adds a touch of elegance.

Slip-Stitch Pattern

(Multiple of 4 sts + 3 sts)

Sl all sts pw.

Row 1 (RS): K1, sl 1 wyib, *K3, sl 1 wyib; rep from * to last st, K1.

Row 2: P1, sl 1 wyif, *P3, sl 1 wyif; rep from * to last st, P1.

Row 3: *K3, sl 1 wyib; rep from * to last 3 sts, K3.

Row 4: *P3, sl 1 wyif; rep from * to last 3 sts, P3.

Rep rows 1–4 for patt.

Color Sequence

2 rows with B.

2 rows with C.

2 rows with A.

Rep sequence for patt.

Scarf Instructions

Carry unused yarn up side of work. Do not cut yarn after color change.

With A, use cable CO method (page 59) to CO 321 sts.

Work scallop edging as follows.

Row 1 (WS): Purl.

Row 2: K2, *K1 and sl st just made back onto LH needle, using RH needle lift next 8 sts, 1 at a time, over this st and off needle, YO twice, knit first st on LH needle again, K2; rep from * to end of row.

Row 3: K1, *P2tog, drop first YO of previous row, (K1, P1, K1, P1) into second YO from previous row, P1; rep from * to last st, K1—176 sts.

Row 4: *K43, K1f&b; rep from * 2 more times, K44—179 sts.

Row 5: Knit.

Patt rows: Work in sl-st patt until piece measures 9", ending with even-numbered row in color A. Cont with A only, work 8 more rows of patt.

Next 3 rows: Knit.

Next row (WS): Purl.

BO all sts loosely.

Finishing

Mist to smooth and even the sts.

With RS facing you and A, join yarn at RH corner of short straight edge and work 1 row of sc (page 31) from right to left along 3 straight edges. Do not turn, work 1 row of reverse hdc (at right) from left to right along 3 straight edges. Fasten off. Weave in all ends and mist again slightly.

CROCHETED EDGING

Single crochet. *Working from right to left with RS facing you, attach yarn in first st, *insert hook into next st, yarn over hook, pull loop through to front, yarn over hook, and pull loop through both loops on hook. Repeat from * to end.*

Keeping edges flat: *It's important to space crochet stitches carefully so the edges of the piece lie flat. The formula for spacing stitches on a vertical edge is to work into each knot at the edge. For a horizontal row, the formula is one crochet stitch for every one and a half knit stitches; go into a stitch, then between the next two stitches, and repeat across the row. However, even using the formula as a guide, it may be necessary to skip or add stitches to keep the edge flat.*

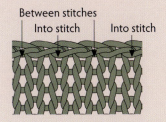

Reverse half double crochet. *Working from left to right with RS facing you, *yarn over hook, insert hook into next st at right, yarn over hook, pull through loop to front, yarn over hook, and pull loop through all 3 loops on hook. Repeat from * to end.*

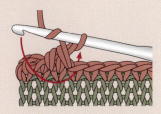

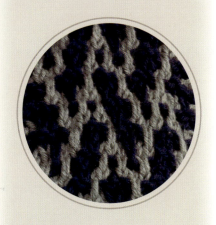

TOKEN CREEK

Show a token amount of attitude by wearing a skinny little scarf with a textured slip-stitch pattern and narrow ruffled ends—perfect for year-round styling.

FINISHED MEASUREMENTS

5" x 37"

MATERIALS

Jeanee from Plymouth Yarn Company, Inc. (51% cotton, 49% acrylic; 50 g; 111 yds)

(4)

A 1 skein in color 01 (light gray)

B 1 skein in color 57 (dark blue)

Size 10 (6 mm) needles or size required to obtain gauge

2 stitch markers

GAUGE

20 sts = 4" in sl-st patt

Slip-Stitch Pattern

(Multiple of 8 sts + 3 sts)

Sl all sts pw.

Row 1 (RS): With A, K1, *K2, sl 1 wyib, K3, sl 2; rep from * to 2 sts before marker, K2.

Rows 2, 6, 10, and 14: With A, purl the purl sts and sl the slipped sts wyif.

Row 3: With B, K1, *(K1, sl 1 wyib) 3 times, K2; rep from * to 2 sts before marker, K2.

Rows 4, 8, and 12: With B, knit the purl sts and slip the slipped sts wyif.

Row 5: With A, K1, *sl 1 wyib, K3, sl 1 wyib, K2, sl 1 wyib; rep from * to 2 sts before marker, sl 1 wyib, K1.

Row 7: With B, K1, *K2, sl 1 wyib, K3, sl 1 wyib, K1; rep from * to 2 sts before marker, K2.

Row 9: With A, K1, *sl 1 wyib, K2, sl 2 wyib, K3; rep from * to 2 sts before marker, K2.

Row 11: With B, K1, *K1, sl 1 wyib, K3, sl 1 wyib, K1, sl 1 wyib; rep from * to 2 sts before marker, K2.

Row 13: With A, K1, *K2, sl 2 wyib, K2, sl 1 wyib, K1; rep from * to 2 sts before marker, K2.

Row 15: With B, K1, *sl 1 wyib, K3, sl 1 wyib, K3; rep from * to 2 sts before marker, K2.

Row 16: With B, knit the purl sts and sl the slipped sts wyif.

Rep rows 1–16 for patt.

The cast-on and bound-off edges sport a trendy narrow ruffle.

Scarf Instructions

Carry unused yarn up side of work. Do not cut yarn after color change.

With A, CO 75.

Row 1 (RS): Knit.

Row 2: Purl.

Row 3: Knit.

Row 4 (dec row): P3tog across—25 sts.

Row 5: With B, knit.

Row 6 (setup row): With A, K3, pm, purl to last 3 sts, pm, K3.

Patt rows: Knitting first 3 sts and last 3 sts on all rows, work sl-st patt between markers until piece measures 36", ending with row 16.

Next row (RS inc): With A, knit into front, back, and front of each st across—75 sts.

Next row: Purl.

Next row: Knit.

Next row: Purl.

BO all sts loosely.

Finishing

Weave in all ends. Block by misting lightly to smooth and even the sts.

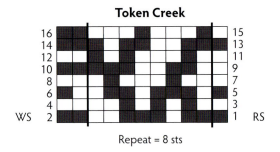

Token Creek

WS 2   1 RS

Repeat = 8 sts

Legend

Sl all sts pw

■ = **A.** When first st in row is black, work sts as follows:
RS: K black squares, sl white squares wyib
WS: P black squares, sl white squares wyif

□ = **B.** When first st in row is white, work sts as follows:
RS: K white squares, sl black squares wyib
WS: K white squares, sl black squares wyif

COWLS

QUARRY HILL CIRCLE

Stay warm and look good as you travel around town wearing this color-banded long cowl. The extra length means more styling options; the soft tweed yarn is a dream to work and to wear.

FINISHED MEASUREMENTS

5" x 94"

MATERIALS

Monte Donegal by Plymouth Yarn Company, Inc. (40% alpaca, 40% merino wool, 14% acrylic, 6% rayon; 50 g; 109 yds)

A 2 skeins in color 500 Black

B 2 skeins in color 5866 Flame

Size 8 (5 mm) circular needle (29" or longer) or size required to obtain gauge

Size 9 (5.5 mm) needle or 1 size larger than needle for gauge for BO only

Size H-5 (5 mm) crochet hook

GAUGE

16 sts = 4" with size 8 needle in sl-st patt

Slip-Stitch Pattern

(Multiple of 16 sts + 3 sts)

Sl all sts pw.

Row 1 (RS): With A, K1, *K3, sl 1 wyib, K12; rep from * to last 2 sts, end K2.

Row 2 and all WS rows: With color from previous row, purl the purl sts and sl the slipped sts wyif.

Row 3: With B, K1, *K2, sl 1 wyib, K1, sl 1 wyib, K11; rep from * to last 2 sts, end K2.

Row 5: With A, K1, *(K1, sl 1 wyib) 3 times, K5, sl 1 wyib, K4; rep from * to last 2 sts, end K2.

Row 7: With B, K1, *(sl 1 wyib, K1) 3 times, sl 1 wyib, K3, sl 1 wyib, K1, sl 1 wyib, K3, rep from * to last 2 sts, sl 1 wyib, K1.

Row 9: With A, K1, *(K1, sl 1 wyib) twice, K5, (sl 1 wyib, K1) 3 times, sl 1 wyib; rep from * to last 2 sts, K2.

Row 11: With B, K1, *sl 1 wyib, K1, sl 1 wyib, K3, (sl 1 wyif, K1) 3 times, sl 1 wyib, K3; rep from * to last 2 sts, sl 1 wyif, K1.

Row 13: With A, K1, *K1, sl 1 wyib, K5, (sl 1 wyib, K1) twice, sl 1 wyib, K4; rep from * to last 2 sts, K2.

Row 15: With B, K1, *K8, sl 1 wyib, K1, sl 1 wyib, K5; rep from * to last 2 sts, K2.

Row 17: With A, K1, *K9, sl 1 wyib, K6; rep from * to last 2 sts, K2.

Row 18: With A, purl the purl sts and sl the slipped sts wyif.

Cowl Instructions

Carry unused yarn up side of work. Do not cut yarn after color change.

With A, CO 371 as follows: Place slipknot on crochet hook and hold in RH, hold needle in LH. Place hook on top of needle with yarn below needle, hold yarn with finger of LH. *Catch yarn and pull lp over hook and through lp on hook. Bring working yarn to back under needle. Repeat from * until 370 sts on needle. Sl lp from hook onto needle—371 sts on needle. *Do not join,* patt is worked back and forth in rows.

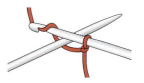

Row 1 (WS): With A, purl.

Rows 2 and 3: With B, knit.

Row 4: Purl.

Row 5: Knit.

Rows 6 and 7: Purl.

Rows 8–25: With A, work 18 rows of sl-st patt once.

Rows 26 and 27: With B, knit.

Row 28: Purl.

Row 29: Knit.

Rows 30 and 31: Purl.

Row 32: With A, knit.

With larger needle, BO all sts loosely pw.

Finishing

Block by misting to smooth and even the sts. Seam short edges tog for cowl.

Wrap once, twice, or three times around neck.

Quarry Hill Circle

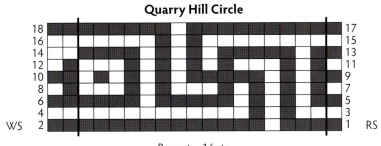

Repeat = 16 sts

Legend

Sl all sts pw

■ = A. When first st in row is black, work sts as follows:
RS: K black squares, sl white squares wyib
WS: P black squares, sl white squares wyif

□ = B. When first st in row is white, work sts as follows:
RS: K white squares, sl black squares wyib
WS: P white squares, sl black squares wyif

MEADOWBROOK LOOP

Worked as a rectangle, twisted, and seamed, this Möbius cowl is sure to become a favorite accessory. Layer it with a T-shirt for a casual look or use it to add some sass to a little black dress.

FINISHED MEASUREMENTS

6" x 32"

MATERIALS

Cleo from Plymouth Yarn Company, Inc. (100% mercerized pima cotton; 50 g; 125 yds) 3

A 1 skein in color 150 Royalist

B 1 skein in color 173 Lime

Size 8 (5 mm) needles or size required to obtain gauge

Cable needle

GAUGE

22 sts = 4" in sl-st patt

Special Abbreviation

C3R: Sl next 2 sts to cn, hold at back of work, K1, K2 from cn.

Slip-Stitch Pattern

(Multiple of 8 sts + 9 sts)

Sl all sts pw.

Row 1 (RS): With B, K7, *C3R, K5; rep from * across to last 2 sts, K2.

Row 2: K2, purl to last st, K2.

Row 3: With A, K2, (K1, sl 1 wyib) twice, K1, *sl 3 wyib, (K1, sl 1) twice, K1; rep from * to last 2 sts, K2.

Row 4: With A, K2, (K1, sl 1 wyib) twice, K1, *sl 3 wyif, (K1, sl 1) twice, K1; rep from * to last 2 sts, K2.

Rep rows 1–4 for patt.

Cowl Instructions

Carry unused yarn up side of work. Do not cut yarn after color change.

With A, CO 33 sts.

First row (WS): Purl.

Patt rows: Work in sl-st patt until piece measures 32", ending with row 4.

Last row: With A, knit.

BO all sts loosely pw.

Finishing

Block by misting to smooth and even the sts.

To create Möbius strip, bring BO edge to CO edge, twist 180°, and seam edges tog.

CANNONBALL TRAIL

Accessorize with a versatile three-button cowl. Fasten all three buttons and wear this cowl under your coat, or leave one or two undone to wear it on top.

FINISHED MEASUREMENTS

10½" x 31"

MATERIALS

Lamb's Pride Superwash from Brown Sheep Company, Inc. (100% wool; 3.5 oz/ 100 g; 200 yds/183m) (4)

A 1 skein in color 168 Rainforest

B 1 skein in color 93 Ocean Sky

Size 9 (5.5 mm) needles or size required to obtain gauge

3 buttons with shank, ⅞" in diameter

2 stitch markers

GAUGE

18 sts = 4" in sl-st patt

Slip-Stitch Pattern

(Multiple of 8 sts + 3 sts)

Sl all sts pw.

Row 1: With A, K1, *K3, sl 1 wyib, K4; rep from * to 2 sts before marker, end K2.

Row 2 and all WS rows: With color from previous row, purl the purl sts and sl the slipped sts wyif.

Row 3: With B, K1, *K2, (sl 1 wyib, K1) twice, sl 1 wyib, K1; rep from * to 2 sts before marker, K2.

Row 5: With A, K1, *K5, sl 1 wyib, K2; rep from * to 2 sts before marker, K2.

Row 7: With B, K1, *sl 1 wyib, K3, (sl 1 wyib, K1) twice; rep from * to 2 sts before marker, end sl 1 wyib, K1.

Row 9: With A, K1, *K7, sl 1 wyib; rep from * to 2 sts before marker, K2.

Row 11: With B, K1, *sl 1 wyib, K1, sl 1 wyib, K3, sl 1 wyib, K1; rep from * to 2 sts before marker, end sl 1 wyib, K1.

Row 13: With A, K1, *K1, sl 1 wyib, K6; rep from * to 2 sts before marker, K2.

Row 15: With B, K1, *(sl 1 wyib, K1) twice, sl 1 wyib, K3; rep from * to 2 sts before marker, sl 1 wyib, K1.

Row 16: With B, purl the purl sts and sl the slipped sts wyif.

Rep rows 1–16 for patt.

Cowl Instructions

Carry unused yarn up side of work. Do not cut yarn after color change.

With A, CO 49 sts.

Rows 1 and 2: Knit.

Row 3 (buttonhole row): K8, work buttonhole as follows: *sl 1 pw wyif, move yarn to back of work,

Buttons with shanks are easier to button and unbutton than flat buttons.

(sl next st, pass previously slipped st over and off needle) twice. Place slipped st back to LH needle, turn, cable CO (page 59) 3 sts, turn, sl first st from LH needle over to RH needle, pass extra CO st over and off needle, pull to tighten*, K12, rep buttonhole from * to *, K12, rep buttonhole from * to *, K8—49 sts).

Rows 4, 5, and 6: Knit.

Row 7: With B, knit.

Row 8: K3, pm, P43, pm, K3.

Patt rows: Using color indicated on chart and beg with row 1, K3, sl marker, work 43 sts from chart, K3. Cont as established, working chart between markers until piece measures approx 30", ending with row 16.

Next 6 rows: With A, knit.

BO all sts loosely.

Finishing

Weave in all ends. Block by misting lightly to smooth and even the sts. Sew buttons in place to correspond with buttonholes.

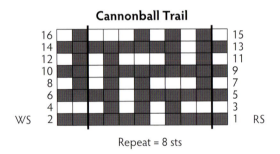

Cannonball Trail

Repeat = 8 sts

Legend

Sl all sts pw

■ = A. When first st in row is black, work sts as follows:
RS: K black squares, sl white squares wyib
WS: P black squares, sl white squares wyif

□ = B. When first st in row is white, work sts as follows:
RS: K white squares, sl black squares wyib
WS: P white squares, sl black squares wyif

SHAWLS

FINISHED MEASUREMENTS

26½" x 53"

MATERIALS

Sahara from Plymouth Yarn Company, Inc. (40% linen, 40% bamboo, 20% silk; 1.75 oz/50 g; 110 yds/100 m)

A 4 skeins in color 1177 (medium green)

B 2 skeins in color 1310 (light green)

Size 10 (6 mm) circular needle (24" long) or size required to obtain gauge

GAUGE

18 sts = 4" in increase garter sl-st patt

MALLOW FLOWER LANE

An elegant wrap that begins at the neck and radiates outward, this half-circle shawl is reversible and drapes beautifully over your shoulders like a gentle hug.

Increase Garter Slip-Stitch Pattern

Sl all sts pw.

Row 1 (inc row, RS): With A (K1, K1f&b) 10 times, K1—31 sts.

Row 2: With A, knit.

Row 3: With B, K2, *sl 1 wyib, K1; rep from * to last st, K1.

Row 4: With B, K2, *sl 1 wyif, K1; rep from * to last 2 sts, K2.

Rep rows 1–4 for patt and AT THE SAME TIME inc as follows on first row of each rep.

Row 5: With A, (K2, K1f&b) 10 times, K1—41 sts.

Row 9: With A, (K3, K1f&b) 10 times, K1—51 sts.

Row 13: With A, (K3, K1f&b, K1) 10 times, K1—61 sts.

Row 17: With A, (K3, K1f&b, K2) 10 times, K1—71 sts.

Row 21: With A, (K4, K1f&b, K2) 10 times, K1—81 sts.

Row 25: With A, (K4, K1f&b, K3) 10 times, K1—91 sts.

Row 29: With A, (K5, K1f&b, K3) 10 times, K1—101 sts.

Row 33: With A, (K5, K1f&b, K4) 10 times, K1—111 sts.

Row 37: With A, (K6, K1f&b, K4) 10 times, K1—121 sts.

Row 41: With A, (K6, K1f&b, K5) 10 times, K1—131 sts.

Row 45: With A, (K7, K1f&b, K5) 10 times, K1—141 sts.

Row 49: With A, (K7, K1f&b, K6) 10 times, K1—151 sts.

Row 53: With A, (K8, K1f&b, K6) 10 times, K1—161 sts.

Row 57: With A, (K8, K1f&b, K7) 10 times, K1—171 sts.

Row 61: With A, (K9, K1f&b, K7) 10 times, K1—181 sts.

The garter-band bind off creates a finished border along the curved bottom edge.

Row 65: With A, (K9, K1f&b, K8) 10 times, K1—191 sts.

Row 69: With A, (K10, K1f&b, K8) 10 times, K1—201 sts.

Row 73: With A, (K10, K1f&b, K9) 10 times, K1—211 sts.

Row 77: With A, (K11, K1f&b, K9) 10 times, K1—221 sts.

Row 81: With A, (K11, K1f&b, K10) 10 times, K1—231 sts.

Row 85: With A, (K12, K1f&b, K10) 10 times, K1—241 sts.

Row 89: With A, (K12, K1f&b, K11) 10 times, K1—251 sts.

Row 93: With A, (K13, K1f&b, K11) 10 times, K1—261 sts.

Row 97: With A, (K13, K1f&b, K12) 10 times, K1—271 sts.

Row 101: With A, (K14, K1f&b, K12) 10 times, K1—281 sts.

Row 105: With A, (K14, K1f&b, K13) 10 times, K1—291 sts.

Row 109: With A, (K15, K1f&b, K13) 10 times, K1—301 sts.

Row 113: With A, (K15, K1f&b, K14) 10 times, K1—311 sts.

Row 117: With A, (K16, K1f&b, K14) 10 times, K1—321 sts.

Row 121: With A, (K16, K1f&b, K15) 10 times, K1—331 sts.

Shawl Instructions

Sl all sts pw.

Carry unused yarn up side of work. Do not cut yarn after color change. A circular needle is required to accommodate large number of sts. Do NOT join. Work back and forth in rows.

With A, CO 3 sts.

Setup rows:

Row 1 (WS): With A, knit.

Row 2 (RS): K1f&b across—6 sts.

Row 3: Knit.

Row 4: With B, K2, sl 1 wyib, K3.

Row 5: With B, K3, sl 1 wyif, K2.

Row 6: With A, K1f&b across—12 sts.

Row 7: Knit.

Row 8: With B, K2, *sl 1 wyib, K1; rep from * to last 2 sts, K2.

Row 9: With B, K3, *sl 1 wyif, K1; rep from * to last st, K1.

Row 10: With A, K1, (K1f&b) 9 times, K2—21 sts.

Row 11: Knit.

Row 12: With B, K2, *sl 1 wyib, K1; rep from * to last st, K1.

Row 13: With B, K2, *sl 1 wyif, K1; rep from * to last 2 sts, K1.

Patt rows: Work in increase garter sl-st patt until there are 331 sts, ending with row 4.

Next 2 rows: With A, knit 2 rows.

Work garter BO as follows: Using cable CO method (page 59), CO 5 sts. *K4, K2tog tbl, turn, K5; rep from * until 5 sts rem on RH needle, turn, BO rem 5 sts in usual manner.

Finishing

Weave in all ends carefully so that piece is reversible and can be worn with either side showing. Block by misting lightly to smooth and even the sts.

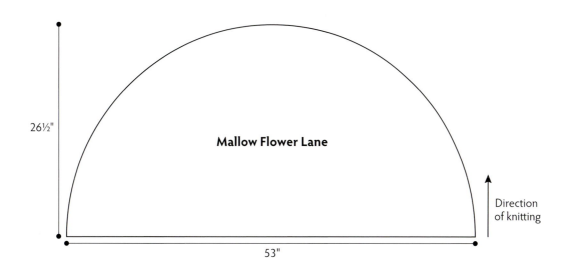

Mallow Flower Lane

26½"

53"

Direction of knitting

MORAINE VIEW

Arrive in style wearing this reversible shoulder wrap trimmed with sequin-tipped fringe. Let your inner diva shine and shimmer as you enjoy the compliments.

FINISHED MEASUREMENTS

18" x 70"

MATERIALS

Vipe from Dale Garn (100% mercerized Egyptian cotton; 1.75 oz/50 g; 136 yds/125 m)

- **A** 2 skeins in color 5752 Slate
- **B** 1 skein in color 20 Natural

Size 11 (8 mm) needles or size required to obtain gauge

2 packages (.71 oz/20 g) of black 20 mm flat, round sequins

Sewing needle with large eye

GAUGE

15 sts = 4" in sl-st patt

Increase Slip-Stitch Pattern

(Multiple of 2 sts + 1 st)

Sl all sts pw.

Row 1 (RS): With A, knit to last st, K1f&b.

Row 2: K1f&b, knit to end.

Row 3: With B, K1, *sl 1 wyib, K1; rep from * to end of row.

Row 4: Knit.

Rep rows 1–4 for inc sl-st patt.

Even Slip-Stitch Pattern

(Multiple of 2 sts + 1 st)

Sl all sts pw.

Rows 1 (RS) and 2: With A, knit.

Row 3: With B, K1, *sl 1 wyib, K1; rep from * to end of row.

Row 4: Knit.

Rep rows 1–4 for even sl-st patt.

Decrease Slip-Stitch Pattern

(Multiple of 2 sts + 1 st)

Sl all sts pw.

Row 1 (RS): With A, knit to last 3 sts, K2tog, K1.

Row 2: K2tog, knit to end of row.

Row 3: With B, K1, *sl 1 wyib, K1; rep from * to end of row.

Row 4: Knit.

Rep rows 1–4 for dec sl-st patt.

Shawl Instructions

Carry unused yarn up side of work. Do not cut yarn after color change.

With A, CO 3 sts.

Rows 1 (RS) and 2: Knit 2 rows.

Inc sl-st patt rows: Work inc sl-st patt until piece measures approx 30" when slightly stretched, ending with row 4.

Even sl-st patt rows: Work even sl-st patt for 10", ending with row 4.

Dec sl-st patt rows: Work dec sl-st patt until 3 sts rem on needle, ending with row 2.

Next 2 rows: With A, knit.

BO all sts loosely.

Finishing

Block by misting to smooth and even the stitches. Weave in all ends.

Fringe: Cut 134 strands, each 10" long. With sewing needle, thread 2 sequins onto each strand. Make overhand knot at each end and slide a sequin to each edge. Attach 1 fringe (see page 60) to every other row along sides and bottom edge. Fringe can be applied without sequins for a less flashy look. To untangle sequin-tipped fringe, hold shawl along top neck edge with both hands and shake firmly. Any remaining tangles can easily be combed out with your fingers.

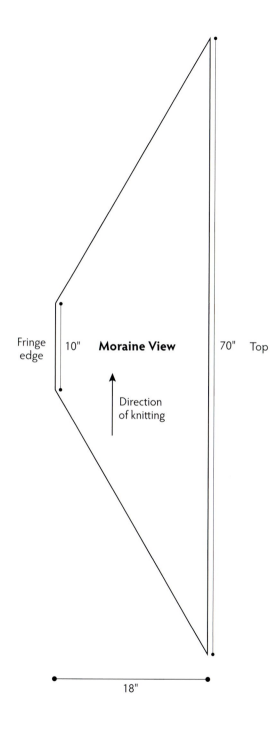

Fringe
edge

10"

Moraine View

70" Top

↑

Direction
of knitting

18"

*Create fabulous fringe by adding
flat, round sequins.*

YAHARA BAY

Keep things casual with this fringe-trimmed wrap. Imagine the varying hues of blue water gently washing over your shoulders and enjoy the year-round comfort.

FINISHED MEASUREMENTS

14" x 62", excluding fringe

MATERIALS

Cotton Fleece from Brown Sheep Company, Inc. (80% cotton, 20% merino wool; 3.5 oz/ 100 g; 215 yds/197 m) (4)

- **A** 2 skeins in color CW105 Putty
- **B** 1 skein in color CW360 Wild Sage
- **C** 1 skein in color CW400 New Age Teal
- **D** 1 skein in color CW385 Deep Sea Fog

Size 7 (4.5 mm) needles or size required to obtain gauge

Size H-8 (5 mm) crochet hook

GAUGE

17 sts = 4" in ribbon patt

Ribbon Pattern

(Multiple of 4 sts + 3 sts)

Sl all sts pw.

Cut yarn after each use; do NOT carry yarn up side. When starting a new color, firmly tie a square knot around the 8" cut tail, leaving an 8" tail of the new color, and slide knot up to first st on needle. The beg and end tails make up the fringe on one side.

Row 1 (RS): With A, knit.

Row 2: With A, purl. Cut A, leaving 8" tail.

Row 3: With B, K1, *sl 1 wyib, K3; rep from * to last 2 sts, sl 1 wyib, K1.

Row 4: With B, P1, *sl 1 wyif, P3; rep from * to last 2 sts, sl 1 wyif, P1. Cut B, leaving 8" tail.

Row 5: With A, knit.

Row 6: With A, purl. Cut A, leaving 8" tail.

Row 7: With C, K3, *sl 1 wyif, K3; rep from * to end.

Row 8: With C, P3, *sl 1 wyib, P3; rep from * to end.

Row 9: With C, K3, *sl 1 wyif, K3; rep from * to end.

Row 10: With C, P3, *sl 1 wyib, P3; rep from * to end. Cut C, leaving 8" tail.

Row 11: With A, knit.

Row 12: With A, purl. Cut A, leaving 8" tail.

Row 13: With B, K1, *sl 1 wyib, K3; rep from * to last 2 sts, sl 1 wyib, K1.

Row 14: With B, P1, *sl 1 wyif, P3; rep from * to last 2 sts, sl 1 wyif, P1. Cut B, leaving 8" tail.

Row 15: With A, knit.

Row 16: With A, purl. Cut A, leaving 8" tail.

Row 17: With D, K3, *sl 1 wyib, K3; rep from * to end.

Row 18: With D, P3, *sl 1 wyif, P3; rep from * to end.

Row 19: With D, K3, *sl 1 wyib, K3; rep from * to end.

Row 20: With D, P3, *sl 1 wyif, P3; rep from * to end. Cut D, leaving 8" tail.

Rep rows 1–20 for patt.

Shawl Instructions

With B, cable CO (page 59) 271 sts, leaving 8" tail at beg.

Row 1 (RS): Purl.

Row 2: Knit.

Row 3: Purl.

Rows 4–103: Work 20-row ribbon patt a total of 5 times.

Rows 104–109: Rep rows 1–6 of ribbon patt.

Row 110 (RS): With B, knit.

Row 111: Knit.

Row 112: Purl.

Row 113: Knit.

Work P2tog, BO loosely on RS as follows: P1, *sl st back to left needle wyif, P2tog; rep from * until all sts are bound off.

Enjoy the rhythm of this stitch pattern and imagine the waves washing ashore.

Finishing

Weave in all ends.

Fringe: Cut 16"-long strands as follows:

 22 strands from A

 11 strands from B

 15 strands from C

 15 strands from D

Along edge *without* tails, starting with first B stripe, apply 1 fringe (page 60) every 2 rows, matching fringe color to color of knit stripe, ending with last stripe B—53 fringes applied.

Along edge *with* tails, apply additional fringe as follows:

 Add 1 fringe of C to each C stripe—5 fringes applied.

 Add 1 fringe of D to each D stripe—5 fringes applied.

Trim fringe to even lengths.

Block by misting lightly to smooth and even the sts.

Start and Finish Like a Pro

The instructions in this book assume some basic knitting knowledge, but a few special techniques are explained here for your convenience.

Cable Cast On

Make a slipknot and place on a needle. Knit into the loop and place the resulting stitch on the left needle by inserting the left needle into the stitch from the right side of the loop. *Insert the right needle between the two stitches, wrap the yarn around the needle, pull the new loop through to the front, and place it on the left needle. Repeat from * for the specified number of stitches.

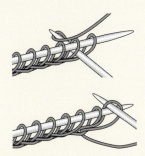

Joining a New Ball of Yarn

Whenever possible, attach a new ball of yarn at the beginning of the row. Tie the new strand onto the old tail with a single knot. Slide the new knot up the old tail to the needle and begin knitting with the new yarn. Weave in the tails as you finish the project.

Seams

A few of the projects require seams to join the pieces. There are different ways to make seams, depending on what kind of stitches you're joining.

SEAMING VERTICAL STITCHES TO VERTICAL STITCHES

Work on the right side with wrong sides together and right sides facing out. Insert a tapestry needle threaded with matching yarn under the two strands forming the V that points toward the seam; pull the yarn through and repeat on the other side, working V to V across the seam. The seam should look like a row of knitting. Work carefully and do not pull the yarn too tight.

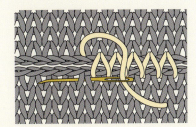

WHIPSTITCH

Hold pieces with right sides together and wrong sides facing out. Insert a tapestry needle threaded with matching yarn just inside the edge of the pieces, pull through, and bring the needle around to the front, ready to insert again. Repeat until the seam is complete, taking care not to seam too tightly. The yarn will appear wrapped around the edges of the pieces.

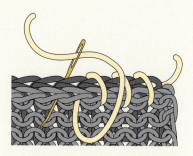

Applying Fringe

Cut the fringe to the specified length. Fold in half. Insert the crochet hook from the front to the back of the work. Catch the folded fringe and pull through the knitted piece, creating a loop. Draw the fringe ends through the loop and pull to tighten. Trim as necessary to even the lengths.

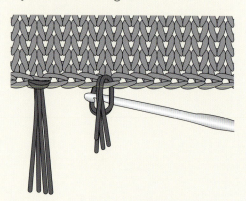

Blocking

First choose a flat, waterproof surface to spread out the piece to be blocked. Blocking boards can be purchased or the top of an ironing board or the floor covered with a towel will work, depending on the size of the project. Regardless of the method used for blocking, the piece should remain in place until dry.

MIST METHOD

Lay the knitted piece on the surface, shaping to the specified dimensions. Fill a clean spray bottle with water and mist lightly. Allow to dry completely before moving.

PIN-AND-MIST METHOD

Lay the knitted piece on the surface and pin the piece to the specified measurements. Fill a clean spray bottle with water and mist heavily. Allow to dry completely before removing pins.

WET METHOD

Dip the knitted piece in cool water. Gently squeeze out the water. Do not wring or twist the piece. Roll the piece in an absorbent bath towel to blot out the excess water. Spread on the surface and pin to specified dimensions. Allow to dry completely before removing the pins or wires.

Useful Information

Standard Yarn-Weight System

Yarn-Weight Symbol and Category Name	🧶 1 Super Fine	🧶 2 Fine	🧶 3 Light	🧶 4 Medium	🧶 5 Bulky	🧶 6 Super Bulky
Types of Yarn in Category	Sock, Fingering, Baby	Sport, Baby	DK, Light Worsted	Worsted, Afghan, Aran	Chunky, Craft, Rug	Bulky, Roving
Knit Gauge Range* in Stockinette Stitch to 4"	27 to 32 sts	23 to 26 sts	21 to 24 sts	16 to 20 sts	12 to 15 sts	6 to 11 sts
Recommended Needle in US Size Range	1 to 3	3 to 5	5 to 7	7 to 9	9 to 11	11 and larger
Recommended Needle in Metric Size Range	2.25 to 3.25 mm	3.25 to 3.75 mm	3.75 to 4.5 mm	4.5 to 5.5 mm	5.5 to 8 mm	8 mm and larger

These are guidelines only. The above reflect the most commonly used gauges and needle sizes for specific yarn categories.

Metric Conversion

Yards	=	meters	x	1.09
Meters	=	yards	x	0.9144
Ounces	=	grams	x	0.035
Grams	=	ounces	x	28.35

Abbreviations and Glossary

approx approximately

beg begin(ning)

BO bind off

cn cable needle(s)

CO cast on

cont continue(ing)(s)

C3R cable 3 right

dec decrease(ing)(s)

g gram

hdc half double crochet

inc increase(ing)(s)

K knit

K1f&b knit into the front and the back of the next stitch—1-stitch increase

K2tog knit two stitches together—1-stitch decrease

LH left hand

lp(s) loop(s)

m meter

mm millimeter

oz ounce

P purl

P2tog purl two stitches together—1-stitch decrease

patt pattern

pm place marker

pw purlwise

rem remain(ing)

RH right hand

RS right side

sc single crochet

sl 1 slip 1 stitch

St st Stockinette stitch

st(s) stitch(es)

tbl through back loop

tog together

WS wrong side

wyib with yarn in back

wyif with yarn in front

yds yards

YO yarn over

Resources

Contact the following companies to locate the yarns and supplies used in this book.

Brown Sheep Company, Inc.
www.brownsheep.com
Cotton Fleece
Lamb's Pride Superwash

Denise Interchangeable Needles
www.knitdenise.com
Knitting needles

Lion Brand Yarns
www.lionbrand.com
Amazing
*Martha Stewart Crafts Extra
    Soft Wool Blend*

Mango Moon Yarns
www.mangomoonyarns.com
Dale Garn Falk
Dale Garn Lille Lerke
Dale Garn Vipe
Di Lusso

Plymouth Yarn Company, Inc.
www.plymouthyarn.com
Cleo
Encore
Jeanee
Monte Donegal
Sahara

Acknowledgments

My heartfelt thanks go to:

Barbara Walker, knitting luminary, who developed this color technique.

Mary Green and Karen Soltys, leaders of the editorial team at Martingale, for believing in this concept and for your support.

Ursula Reikes, my technical editor, who can navigate through my chaos without losing her good humor; your attention to detail is unrivaled.

The entire team at Martingale. You are all incredibly talented and a joy to work with. I appreciate your dedication, enthusiasm, and efforts on behalf of my books.

Brown Sheep Company, Lion Brand Yarns, Mango Moon Yarns, and Plymouth Yarn Company for generously providing yarn for the projects.

Cia and Vanessa at Plymouth for your timely attention to my last-minute request for color changes.

Linda and Emily at Denise Interchangeable Needles for your support.

Ruth for sharing your talent and love for knitting.

Kevin, my husband, for your encouragement.

About the Author

SHERYL THIES retired from a career in health care to follow her artistic passion—combining fiber, texture, and color. In addition to designing and teaching both knitting and Tunisian crochet, she enjoys traveling and spending time outdoors. She can often be found on the bocce court, either playing or refereeing. She is the author of several Martingale books and lives near Madison, Wisconsin, with her husband.